The Breath of Life

David Hare is one of Britain's most internationally performed playwrights. Born in Sussex in 1947, he had a long association with Britain's National Thatre, which produced eleven of his plays successively between 1978 and 1997. A trilogy about the church, the law and the Labour Party – *Racing Demon, Murmuring Judges* and *The Absence of War* – was presented in repertory at the Olivier Theatre in 1993. Nine of his best-known plays, including *Plenty, The Secret Rapture, Skylight, The Blue Room, Amy's View, The Judas Kiss* and *Via Dolorosa* – in which he performed – have also been presented on Broadway.

DAVID HARE

The Breath of Life

faber and faber

First published in 2002
by Faber and Faber Limited
3 Queen Square London WC1N 3AU
Published in the United States by Faber and Faber Inc.
an affiliate of Farrar, Straus and Giroux LLC, New York

Typeset by Country Setting, Kingsdown, Kent CT14 8ES
Printed in England by Mackays of Chatham plc, Chatham, Kent

© David Hare, 2002

A CIP record for this book
is available from the British Library

ISBN 0-571-21593-9

2 4 6 8 10 9 7 5 3 1

For Nicole, with love

The Breath of Life was first presented at the Theatre Royal, Haymarket, London, on 4 October 2002, produced by Robert Fox. The cast was as follows:

Frances Judi Dench
Madeleine Maggie Smith

Director Howard Davies
Designer William Dudley
Lighting Designer Hugh Vanstone

Characters

Frances Beale
Madeleine Palmer

THE BREATH OF LIFE

Life being what it is, one dreams of revenge.
Gauguin

One

Day. A first-floor flat in a huge Victorian stone terrace on an English seafront. A stretch of crumbling high windows give onto an expanse of sky, and to the unseen sea beyond. The sound of seagulls. The room is filled with a grey, lowering afternoon light. An unnaturally large room serves as everything – kitchen, living room, work room. Beneath the windows runs a long continuous window-seat. The room is archived with ranges of high wide shelves which contain the life's study of Madeleine Palmer.

Madeleine is opening the door of the flat. She is in her early sixties with auburn hair. Frances Beale is standing outside, fair-haired, a little younger, plumper, softer, a pale-beige coat wrapped tightly around her.

Frances You don't mind? I'm not imposing? I rang. I did ring.

Madeleine I know you rang. Why are you telling me you rang? I'm not so old, I hope I can still remember a phone call.

Frances I wouldn't have just burst in.

Madeleine Oh, and that makes it all right, does it?

Frances No.

Madeleine Giving warning makes it all right?

Neither woman has moved. Frances is still standing outside.

Frances So this is how you are in life.

There is a moment's silence.

Madeleine What's the plan? You're going to stand there all day?

Frances is still frozen to the spot.

Are you going to take your coat off?

Frances Thank you.

Madeleine You're welcome.

Frances comes tentatively into the flat. Madeleine closes the door behind her.

Frances It's sort of a time-slip, isn't it?

Madeleine What is?

Frances Oh, not us, I'm not meaning us. I'm meaning the place. It's a fascinating choice. Do you know I've never been before?

Madeleine Well, you can't pass through.

Frances No.

Madeleine It doesn't *go* anywhere. And as for choice, no, more that it's cheap, not a choice. (*Madeleine has crossed the room and is making no more effort to welcome Frances.*)

Frances A part of England that's still England, I mean.

Madeleine You sound as if you disapprove.

The two women look at each other a moment.

Are you going to take your coat off and sit down?

Frances Not yet.

Frances makes an effort to be conciliatory.

Frances This is my fault, I know. It's my idea. It's not spontaneous. I have to say, it's a year now, I've been meaning to come and see you.

Madeleine Really?

Frances Yes. On a question of literary ethics.

Madeleine Literary?

Frances Yes.

Madeleine One of your novels?

Frances No, not one of my novels . . .

Madeleine Good . . .

Frances . . . as it happens . . .

Madeleine I've always suspected that I was going to turn up as a character one day.

Frances Well, you're not. Not in a novel, anyway.

Madeleine looks at her, unyielding.

And what's more, if you did, I don't know how you'd ever find out.

Madeleine No doubt somebody would tell me. My experience, there's always someone eager to bring you bad news.

There is a slight thaw between them for the first time. Frances looks at the overflowing shelves.

Frances You've been here long?

Madeleine Three years.

Frances You have everything.

Madeleine Yes. My whole life.

Frances And do you go to the mainland?

5

Madeleine Not much.

Frances It must be hard to get books. What do you do? Order on the internet?

Madeleine shifts.

Madeleine Frances, I'm telling you, believe me, when you rang to say you wanted to see me, I agreed. Here you are. Really, it's fine. But at least tell me the reason.

There is a brief silence.

Frances Well, it's to do with Martin.

Madeleine So?

Frances Indirectly.

Madeleine Where is he?

Frances Where *is* he?

Madeleine Yes.

Frances Seattle.

Madeleine shrugs slightly.

Madeleine Well, at least they have earthquakes in Seattle.

Frances So they say.

Madeleine And huge tidal waves. All in all, it seems quite a hopeful environment.

Frances You didn't know? He doesn't write?

Madeleine Where is he? A log-cabin in the woods? Does he still work? What does he do?

Frances Martin?

Madeleine I haven't actually said his name in a while. At least not out loud. 'Martin.' (*She looks at Frances a moment.*) What would you like? Tea?

But Frances ignores the question.

Frances People treat me as if I were in the full flood of suffering. It's hard to explain, I've done my suffering. It's over. 'Oh,' they say, 'but you must be so hurt.' I was hurt. I'm not hurt any more.

Madeleine You have a life.

Frances Well, that's it. I have plenty to get on with.

Madeleine I don't have a television, but I know that if I did, I'd see you all the time.

Frances You'd see me. (*Frances smiles.*) Martin mentioned that.

Madeleine What?

Frances That you disdained television.

Madeleine 'Disdained'? That's a strong word. I just don't have one, that's all.

Frances Why not?

Madeleine is impatient.

Madeleine Look, why don't we leave this sort of thing? I'm out of practice. What is it Americans say? 'I don't use that muscle any more.'

Frances Which muscle is that?

Madeleine The one that works my mouth.

Frances What are you saying? You mean you don't speak?

Madeleine Hardly.

Frances Is that through choice?

Madeleine It's not a vow, if that's what you're asking. There's no religious dimension.

Frances Aren't you lonely?

Madeleine makes a wintry smile.

Madeleine No, I haven't heard from him and no, he doesn't write. Why would he?

Frances I thought perhaps you kept in touch.

Madeleine Martin never wrote, as far as I know. He scrawled little notes, didn't he?

Frances Yes.

Madeleine Those little yellow post-its occasionally. 'Had to go. Martin.' 'See you.' 'About last night: I'm sorry, I promise I'll never do it again.' But a whole letter, no, never. Did he write to you?

Frances Well, he had no need, did he? (*Frances shifts a little, coming into the room.*) And I don't get up every morning looking for the Seattle postmark, if that's what you're asking.

Madeleine No.

Frances Far from it.

Madeleine Is he allowed to practise?

Frances I imagine.

Madeleine Is it like a driving licence? You can do it in any country?

Frances I don't actually know.

Madeleine Aren't their laws different from ours?

Frances I think they take the law more seriously than we do.

Madeleine Yes, loads more of them and everyone in court all the time.

8

Frances As if it could help. That's the difference. They think the law can help.

Madeleine I think they just want to win, don't they?

Frances Do you think that's what it is?

Madeleine Of course. They like concrete victories. And a court's as good a place as any. (*Madeleine relaxes, starting to unbend.*) Do you think that's why Martin went?

Frances I don't think so.

Madeleine Status?

Frances Unlikely.

Madeleine Do you think status is what Martin wanted? After all, lawyers are like priests over there. In America. Is that what drew him? Maybe he felt he could be nearer the centre of things.

Frances Martin . . .

They both smile at the unlikelihood of it.

Madeleine It always leaps out at me . . .

Frances What does?

Madeleine When you read in the paper: 'American lives have been lost . . . '

Frances Oh yes.

Madeleine Their politicians always put on that tone of special shock. 'This situation endangers American lives.' As if American lives were automatically different from any other kind, in a different category, a different *category* of life . . .

Frances But isn't that what they believe?

Madeleine That's how they are. Because they're richer than everyone else, so they have to insist their dramas are more significant. (*Madeleine shakes her head.*) And my God, all that behaviour in restaurants . . .

Frances What behaviour?

Madeleine Even here, even on the island, you hear them in restaurants . . .

Frances Who?

Madeleine Americans.

Frances Oh.

Madeleine 'Does this chicken have skin on it?' What's all that about?

Frances You tell me.

Madeleine This incredible fear. This terror. What's the waiter meant to say?

Frances I don't know.

Madeleine 'No, this chicken never had a skin. This chicken shivered skinless in its coop at night, just pure flesh and feather, terrified it might one day give an American a calorie.'

Frances Well, quite.

Madeleine I mean, somebody tell me: are the two connected? How are they connected? At once the most powerful people on earth and now it appears the most fearful . . .

Frances Perhaps that's why.

Madeleine The most risk-averse. (*Madeleine is emphatic, summing up.*) Life with all the life taken out of it.

Frances Perhaps they just feel they have more to lose.

Madeleine looks at her, unforgiving.

Madeleine Well, they don't.

Frances Of course not.

Madeleine They'll die like we die.

Frances Well, yes. (*Frances frowns slightly.*) I mean, not quite.

Madeleine Oh, maybe with a few more drips attached . . .

Frances That's what I meant . . .

Madeleine Yes, with a few more monitors, perhaps. Jumping up in their beds like rubber dolls when the electrodes are applied. A couple more weeks of gibbering half-consciousness. Parked for a while in some chemical waiting room. Yes, they'll get that. Electronically bestowed. Death delayed but not denied. But finally, no: they'll lose what we lose. (*Madeleine nods bitterly.*) Take it from me.

Frances Well, I will. (*Frances smiles slightly.*) You seem to have thought about it.

Madeleine What?

Frances Death.

Madeleine Well, that's hardly surprising, is it?

Frances looks blankly.

Madeleine Look around you. It's the Isle of Wight.

Frances Oh I see . . .

Madeleine Didn't you notice? The whole south coast of England. Gardening and dying. That's what we do. It's a universal impulse, isn't it? Crawl south and expire. Isle of Black, that's what I call it.

Frances is nodding.

Frances No, but also when I came in . . .

Madeleine What?

Frances No, it's interesting.

Madeleine Why?

Frances I thought at the time, when I came in, I thought: the first thing you said, do you remember?

Madeleine No.

Frances Do you remember what you said?

Madeleine Well, I don't.

Frances The very first thing. 'I hope I'm not so *old*,' you said. At once you said 'old'.

Madeleine is irritated.

Madeleine Oh I see, yes, of course, I'd forgotten, this is novelist's notebook, is it?

Frances Not at all. I'm just saying.

Madeleine It all gets stored away. Foolish. So significant for us to meet each other and my mistake was to think we were going to have a conversation . . .

Frances We were. We are.

Madeleine I had this idea we were simply *talking* to one another. But, of course, I'd forgotten in your new line of work it's all evidence isn't it? It's all booty.

Frances No.

Madeleine Any unguarded remark and at once Tolstoy here puts it in the computer.

Frances That's not what I meant.

Madeleine Isn't it?

Frances No.

Madeleine Drop by, take down what the victim says, pop her in the oven in a lightly buttered dish, and fifteen minutes later – wow – she's fiction. One character, female. Obviously alone, and apparently anti-American. And scared of dying. Garnish lightly. Serves two.

Frances is not giving ground.

Frances You've always had a problem with fiction, is that right?

Madeleine Yes. As it happens, I have.

Frances I mean, even before I started writing it.

Madeleine Yes.

Frances You never liked it.

Madeleine No.

Frances Why not?

Madeleine I do have a sort of problem with it. I do. Nothing to do with you. More, a fundamental objection.

Frances Which is?

Madeleine Do you want me to say?

Frances Yes.

Madeleine looks at her a moment.

Madeleine Oh. That it isn't true.

There is a silence. Frances watches, a little chastened, as Madeleine now moves away. She speaks quietly.

That's all.

Frances Ah.

Madeleine Silly, isn't it?

Frances No. Not if that's what you feel.

Madeleine It is.

Frances Fair enough.

Madeleine Well that's it. That's all I'm saying. There's more to most of us than books tend to allow. In my own case, for instance, I think there's a little more to me, a little more perhaps than you would see in a novel. I go a little deeper.

Frances Well, of course. That's why I wouldn't put you in a novel.

Madeleine Wouldn't you?

Frances No. At least not without your permission.

They both smile.

Madeleine Thank you.

Frances It's nothing.

Madeleine And so who would you put in?

Frances Oh . . .

Madeleine All your two-dimensional friends?

Frances Of course.

Madeleine Presumably two-dimensional people can go in, people with no depth, presumably they can go in quite easily . . .

Frances They leap in.

Madeleine Good.

There is a moment's silence.

And Martin? Does Martin go in?

Frances looks at her, refusing to reply.

Madeleine The whole point of the world – excuse me, but the thing that makes the world wonderful being its variety –

Frances Well?

Madeleine What's the point of reducing that variety?

Frances Is that what a novelist does?

Madeleine Yes. You consider everything that's in the world, you look at it in all its richness and its difference, and you dare to say, 'Look, it can be reduced to this.' (*Madeleine looks down, as if holding back feeling.*) Tell me, what's the point of that?

Frances Because that's what we do. That's what human beings do anyway. All the time. They select. We're selecting.

Madeleine Judging?

Frances Yeah.

Frances waits, but Madeleine says nothing.

Frances So? That's what the novel is. It's the place where somebody picks out what's important.

Madeleine What's important to them.

Frances Well, certainly. What's wrong with that? Aren't you interested in other people? Don't other people interest you? (*Frances smiles slightly, as if knowing it's a good question.*) That's what the novel's meant to do. Help you imagine what it's like to be someone else. Some people enjoy that, you see. They think it's time well spent. You feel larger. You're not trapped in yourself.

The atmosphere has become tenser, Madeleine knowing that Frances is talking about her.

Frances And just for the record, I don't actually have a computer . . .

Madeleine I'm sorry.

Frances I write by hand.

Madeleine My mistake.

Frances Old school notebooks, in fact. That's what started me. Oddly. I found a stack of exercise books and I started writing. If I hadn't found the books, who knows? (*Frances relaxes a little.*) Some people seem to think it was an act of revenge. It wasn't. 'Making my mark,' people used to say . . .

Madeleine Ugh . . .

Frances Yes, that awful condescending thing people have towards wives at parties. Or therapy. It wasn't that either. The extraordinary thing about writing was that I did it because I liked it.

Madeleine No better reason.

Frances Exactly. Perhaps if I'd started younger it would have been a burden. It would have been a profession. Or an obligation. But it's neither.

Madeleine It was luck.

Frances That's right.

Madeleine That's what you're saying.

Frances Yes.

Madeleine And you hadn't had a lot of luck.

Frances looks at her, then decides to concede.

Frances No.

There is a moment, and then at last Frances comes further into the room.

And the other question? No, I haven't put Martin in a novel. Or rather, I haven't succeeded, because, let's face it, he has more dimensions than most people I've met . . .

Madeleine He has, hasn't he?

Frances Not to mention my own feelings . . .

Madeleine Indeed . . .

Frances Which might – what? – have skewed the portrait . . .

Madeleine Just a little.

Frances Just a little. That's right. The painter's hand is meant to be steady, isn't it?

Madeleine So I believe.

Frances Always paint with a steady hand. If the painter's hand shakes, then the drawback is, it reveals more about the painter than it does about the subject.

Madeleine It's true.

Frances And even I, even I knew enough to know: I won't get him.

There is a short silence, Frances thoughtful.

I won't get him and it wouldn't be fair. (*Frances smiles at a memory.*) I did write one disorganised lawyer, a very minor character, always putting the sweet wrapper in his mouth and throwing the sweet away, that sort of thing. A reviewer immediately called him 'a source of endearing comedy'.

Madeleine Oh God.

Frances Yes. I admit that put up a flag. The flag read: 'Don't do Martin.'

Madeleine I'm sure you were right.

Frances I'm prized, you see, among readers. My readers like my quiet, subversive sense of humour.

Madeleine Well, it's good you can laugh.

Frances Oh yes. The last few years, I've been laughing like a drain. (*Frances shrugs slightly.*) And to be fair, looking back, it's not as if I hadn't been expecting it . . .

Madeleine Is that right?

Frances I'd sensed the end was coming.

Madeleine You foresaw it?

Frances I think so.

Madeleine The way it came?

Frances I think so. (*Frances stops, thinking.*) I don't know. I mean, it's hard to remember, but I think so. Looking back on it, whatever held Martin and me together, whatever that was . . .

Madeleine He loved you.

Frances Yes.

Madeleine It was love.

Frances Well, he did. (*Frances stops again, freshly considering it.*) In a way.

Madeleine Of course he did. I can testify to that. God knows he went on about you enough.

Frances Did he?

Madeleine Yes. At length.

Frances He made comparisons? He compared us?

Madeleine Oh yes. And always to your advantage.

Frances Always?

Madeleine Usually, then. On balance.

Frances smiles, conceding.

Frances Yes, he loved me – what do the French say? – 'after his manner . . .'

Madeleine As you did him.

Frances He loved me. Anyway, whatever. And what's more, at the finish, if I'm really trying to be fair, he did some things as well as he could . . .

Madeleine He left well, did he?

Frances . . . given that there is no good way of doing them. But the truth is I knew all along, in my heart I always knew it was likely to end.

Madeleine You feared it, you mean.

Frances Yes.

Madeleine That's not the same as knowing.

Frances looks at her sharply.

And you had children.

Frances Yes.

Madeleine You have the children.

There is a silence. Neither woman moves.

Frances And you, Madeleine? Did you foresee it?

Madeleine just looks at her, not answering.

Madeleine I think what you said was, you'd come to see me about Martin . . .

Frances Yes.

Madeleine . . . that's what you said . . .

Frances I have.

Madeleine Indeed. But you haven't said why. Specifically.

Frances No. Well, be fair. I haven't even sat down.

Madeleine I did ask you to sit down.

Frances I know. I was frightened.

Madeleine Take off your coat.

At last Frances takes off her coat and lays it down on the sofa.

And I'll make a cup of tea.

Madeleine goes and puts the kettle on the stove. Frances sits down. After a moment Madeleine comes back with cups.

Frances What I really want is to write our story. But not as fiction. I want to write it as a memoir.

Two

*Night. Later the same evening. The lights from the
promenade glow pale and intense from outside the high,
uncurtained windows. A streak of neon sends a
penetrating shaft of colour. Madeleine comes through the
main door, carrying a plastic bag of bottles. She doesn't
turn the light on. She goes to the kitchen area and gets
the bottles out. Frances stirs in front of her. She is laid
out on the sofa, full length, her coat loosely over her.*

Frances What happened?

> *Madeleine doesn't answer, just flips the top off a
> bottle, then comes and sits down with a glass on a
> hard chair. After a few moments, Frances speaks
> again.*

What?

Madeleine You fell asleep.

Frances How did I do that?

Madeleine I have no idea.

> *Frances frowns.*

It's a talent.

Frances Have I missed the boat?

Madeleine By some margin.

Frances Lord.

Madeleine Have a glass of beer, it'll wake you up. It's
Chinese.

But neither woman moves.

Frances What time is it?

Madeleine Ten.

Frances What an extraordinary thing to do. (*Frances is lying on her back, not moving*) It's nerves. It must have been nerves. What else can it be?

Madeleine I've known children do it.

Frances Children, yes. Children fall asleep in response to danger.

Madeleine Was I in danger?

Frances Did we eat?

Madeleine No. We drank a lot of tea but we didn't eat. (*Madeleine sips her beer.*)

Frances It's strange. The strangest thing was: the Queen came to Blackheath.

Madeleine In person?

Frances She was in a mini-skirt.

Madeleine Leather or crochet?

Frances Blue, I think. Royal blue. She kept crossing and uncrossing her legs, as if to say: hey, look at me! I could see her knickers. I gave her some sort of cake and Martin entertained her with a few of his stories.

They both smile.

I think she was bored, but she didn't let on.

Madeleine Well, that's the job, isn't it? They're trained for it.

Frances Good manners, you mean?

Madeleine Dissembling.

Frances looks round.

Frances It's the quiet, is it? That makes one's dreams so intense?

Madeleine gets up silently and goes to the kitchen area to get a second glass.

Martin used to sleep so well. And I could never sleep. I never envied him. I used to lie beside him, look at him, so vulnerable. Thought: you would have to be stupid to sleep as easily as that.

Madeleine But he wasn't, was he?

Frances doesn't answer.

Frances One morning he woke, towards the end, he just woke and said: 'It's true. The older you get, the easier it is to be happy.' He said, 'It must be nature's way of preparing you for death.' Then he said, 'Me, I'd rather be young and unhappy.'

Madeleine As if you could choose. (*Madeleine comes back.*)

Frances Jamie used to wear Martin's wig.

Madeleine Really?

Frances Often.

Madeleine How strange.

Frances When he was about seven. He would come into our bedroom, a horse-hair wig on his head. 'Guilty as charged,' he'd scream. 'Guilty as charged.'

Madeleine Guilty of what?

Frances Not getting up, I suppose.

Madeleine hands her a glass of beer, then goes back to sit down.

Did you meet Jamie?

Madeleine No. Never.

Frances You never met either of them?

Madeleine I once saw them at a distance.

Frances Just saw them? You never spoke to them?

Madeleine looks at her a moment.

Madeleine Does this mean you've started? Are you writing this down?

Frances spreads her arms to indicate: no notebook.

Frances The weird thing is, you're right. People aren't interested in fiction any more.

Madeleine But that's what I said. That's the point I was making.

Frances Stories bore them.

Madeleine It's true.

Frances It's as if the story itself is no longer the point.

Madeleine nods, her own view confirmed.

People watch Marilyn Monroe, they're not thinking, 'Oh this is a wonderful film.' They're thinking, 'While she was making this, she was sleeping with the President.'

Madeleine That's right.

Frances That's what interests them.

Madeleine Of course.

Frances 'She went to fifty-one takes.'

Madeleine Exactly. 'She couldn't remember her lines.'

Frances is watching Madeleine intently.

Frances It's no longer the film . . .

Madeleine No . . .

Frances . . . it's not the film which interests them. It's her.

Madeleine That's right.

Frances Who she is. (*Frances nods, becoming more precise.*) The film? Well, the film's just a piece of wrapping, it's nothing . . .

Madeleine That's right . . .

Frances . . . it's coloured paper – you throw it away, you don't even think about it – because all it docs is gct in the way of what you want.

Madeleine Precisely.

Frances And what you want is access.

Madeleine Quite.

Frances So when you tell a story, it's just a tease. Everything is a tease. The story doesn't matter. Because the real point is who you are. Not even who you are. But who you are underneath.

There is a silence. The air is suddenly charged.

Madeleine Yes. You've got it.

Frances looks at her a moment.

Frances Why Chinese?

Madeleine I don't know. The man in the mini-market said, 'Have the Chinese. It's cheap.'

Frances He's your friend?

Madeleine He has tattoos on his fingers, one letter on each. Like this. W–W–J–D. You ask him a question, he looks at his hand. I asked him one day, what do they stand for? (*Madeleine holds up her hand in imitation.*) He said, 'What Would Jesus Do?'

They both laugh.

Frances Very good . . .

Madeleine And then there's this moment, you know?

Frances Tell me: what sort of moment?

Madeleine There's this moment before you realise, just for a moment you walk down the street – actually this particular time I remember I was yards away, I was about a hundred yards down the street . . .

Frances And? So?

Madeleine . . . still thinking: Martin will love this.

Frances Ah yes.

Madeleine I must tell Martin.

Frances Hmm.

Frances is distant, thoughtful. Madeleine gets up and goes to the window seat. The light from the street falls on her face.

Frances And the light. What is it? Is it a bingo hall?

Madeleine Yes. Except here they still call it housey-housey. (*Madeleine walks again across the room to another chair, making the decision to speak.*) I first met Martin in a bar, did you know this?

Frances No. He never told me.

Madeleine Yes.

Frances Where?

Madeleine In Birmingham. Their Birmingham, not ours. (*Madeleine smiles at the memory.*) There was a stupid sort of argument, there was this ridiculous argument . . .

Frances Between you, you mean?

Madeleine Well, that's right.

Frances What about?

Madeleine I mean, I'd been around a bit. I was older, I was some years older. 'Oh,' he said, 'you're older than me. And you always will be.'

Frances He said that? Martin?

Madeleine I know.

Frances On your first meeting?

Madeleine Those exact words. 'And you always will be.' Rather romantic. In a bar. In Alabama.

Madeleine is lost in thought. Frances reaches for her beer, watching.

Madeleine Anyway, we were there for the civil rights marches.

Frances Ah. So that's when it was.

Madeleine I'd fled England.

Frances Really?

Madeleine Yes. I'd walked out. Got up and left. Why not? Years before, I'd even left home.

Frances Are your parents still alive?

Madeleine Alive? I don't think so. It doesn't seem likely, does it?

Frances You don't regret that? You don't regret not knowing?

They frown, neither understanding the other.

Madeleine So there it was, I fled the country I was born in, I took a Greyhound bus all the way across America and the joke is: there he was in a low-life sort of bar in Alabama. The only white face. Also English.

Frances Charming?

Madeleine Immediately.

Frances Already.

Madeleine Charming already, native charm, and a little bit sleepy, even at that age, that sleepy thing he has . . .

Frances Yes . . .

Madeleine . . . and easy, easy as well, at least easy on the surface . . .

Frances Easy at first.

Madeleine That's it. As if things needn't be difficult, and what's all the fuss about?

Frances Yes.

Madeleine 'What's the problem?'

Frances Oh God. 'What's the problem?' He always did that.

Madeleine Yes.

Frances You start to think there's no problem.

Madeleine Yes.

Frances So you get lulled.

Madeleine 'Space,' he said. I remember quite clearly. It was an expression I'd never heard before. People didn't use it. Not in 1963 and least of all in the civil rights movement. Space was something you explored, not something you wrapped around you. 'What are you doing in America?' 'Oh,' said Martin, 'I need space.'

They both smile.

There you are, you see, you have to imagine it, you have to see this boy in a bar . . .

Frances I can. All too clearly.

Madeleine Tousled, a lot of hair in those days and all over the place. Not telling me, you see, that the blacks were suffering terribly . . .

Frances Quite . . .

Madeleine Not pointing out, you see, the burden of historical injustice, and at last the moment has arrived to sweep that injustice away. He didn't claim, you see, illegally drinking his beer and eating his monkey nuts, he didn't *claim* to have been propelled across the Atlantic . . .

Frances No . . .

Madeleine . . . by some burning sense of social indignation. No. Sitting on a stool, and telling me that he's come all this way because he needs space. (*Madeleine gets up,. indignant.*) Now, well, of course, nowadays, that's how everyone speaks . . .

Frances Oh, sure.

Madeleine Forty years later. That's the assumption everyone makes. Hey, it's the common assumption. As if everything must inevitably, finally be only about yourself . . .

Frances Yes.

Madeleine Nothing out there, nothing real, nothing happening. No events. No actual Negroes being beaten with sticks. No burning buses. Events existing only in so far as they raise the endless, fascinating question of what you feel about those events, how the sticks affect *you*, how the burning buses affect *you* . . . (*Madeleine thinks a moment.*) But me, I'm still young. I'm a prig. I'm sitting beside him getting angry, I'm reaching for my anger – no, actually that's wrong, I've never needed to reach, not for anger, no need to reach, it's there, it's always been there –

Frances You mean even now? Even today?

Madeleine More so. More so today. Yes, ma'am. Angrier than ever.

> *The two women look at each other, then Madeleine goes back to her story.*

'What?' I say. 'You mean you're just here for yourself? No better instincts? No other reasons? No better reasons than that?'

Frances What does he say?

Madeleine Martin? He's not fazed at all. I'm fired up, I'm full of it now. 'You mean you've travelled all this way just for yourself?' 'No,' he says, 'not *just* for myself. Not *only* for myself. If I can help, that's great. But who's to say we shouldn't have a good time helping?'

> *There's a silence, Madeleine thinking.*

Frances Is that when you rowed?

Madeleine No. Later. (*Madeleine has stopped, cutting off her story. Her mood changes.*) That was the time of course the Americans started killing their leaders. The sixties. They had this terror of anyone who might do some good. (*Madeleine gets up to get herself another beer.*)

Frances He never told me that story.

Madeleine Well, he wouldn't, would he? Why would he?

Frances Oh, you'd be surprised. Odd thing: he liked saying your name. He said it a lot.

Madeleine Really?

Frances 'I bumped into that woman today.' 'What woman?' 'What's her name? Oh. Madeleine.'

Madeleine smiles.

Madeleine That's funny.

Frances 'Say it again.' '*Madeleine*. Like the biscuit.' (*Frances smiles as well.*) He seemed to enjoy the risk.

Madeleine You're right. I'm surprised.

There's a moment's silence. Frances shifts on the sofa.

Frances He told me you took him to an orgy.

Madeleine Did he?

Frances Yes.

Madeleine That's what he told you?

Frances Not at the time, of course.

Madeleine Well, it isn't true. I didn't take him to an orgy, I took him to several. I didn't think he was living. I didn't feel he was living. (*Madeleine has become suddenly vehement.*) I took him to a test match as well.

Frances What were they like?

Madeleine Which?

Frances Well, obviously.

Madeleine thinks back a moment.

Madeleine I like orgies. Or I did. But then, finally, it's slightly depressing because they become a hobby, like any other hobby. After a while you see the same people all the time.

Frances I've always wanted to write one.

Madeleine Write one? Oh sure. Well, that just about sums you up, doesn't it?

Frances is suddenly sharper, sitting up.

Frances Oh I see . . .

Madeleine I mean, really!

Frances This is it. Now I understand.

Madeleine Oh please! Really!

Frances Now at least you're being honest. Of course, that's what you've always thought. In your view, that's been my problem all along.

Madeleine Why does there have to be a problem?

Frances Of course there's a *problem*.

Madeleine I'm just saying, all I'm saying is: an orgy isn't meant to be written. You don't *write* an orgy. Of all the things you can do at an orgy that's pretty much the only one that's totally uninteresting.

Frances is nodding, the two of them now exasperated with each other.

Frances Ah well, this is it . . .

Madeleine What is?

Frances What are you saying? You think I'm just family?

Madeleine Well?

Frances You think all I am is family?

Madeleine You are family. That's what you are.

Frances So I was boring family? Yes? Stuck away with the children in Blackheath. And therefore uninteresting. You don't say it, but that's what you mean.

Madeleine He didn't live! I wanted him to live!

Madeleine returns, emphatic, bringing fresh beer. Frances looks at her resentfully.

Madeleine You see, I don't read novels . . .

Frances I know.

Madeleine I don't read what they call female novels. Where they say, oh, there's as much drama in pushing a stroller down the street as there is in fighting a war. They bore me stiff. Because there isn't, you see.

Frances You think that's what I write? You think I write like that?

Madeleine Really, I have no idea what you write, Frances.

Frances Plainly.

Madeleine I'm sure it's all about rich internal lives. Good for you. There's money to be made out of those.

Frances You think it's money I want?

Madeleine I don't see why not.

Frances You think I do it for the money?

Madeleine No. (*Madeleine gets up again and moves across the room. She sits down again.*) You do it to give things significance which don't have significance. That's what you do it for.

There is a silence. Frances is fearful, watching Madeleine closely now.

Frances I'm not sure I follow you.

33

Madeleine Don't you?

Frances No.

Madeleine I think you do. What happens? You get up, you take the kids out, you spend half an hour choosing . . . I don't know, what do you choose? . . . a romper suit. So. Was that time wasted? Was that a life wasted? No, not if you can write about it.

Frances You think that's why I write?

Madeleine looks at her coolly a moment.

Madeleine You came upon writing in later life, you say? I wonder why that was.

Frances I've told you.

Madeleine Have you?

Frances Because I found I had a gift, that's why.

Madeleine Really? Is that the reason?

Frances Yes. (*Frances stops a moment.*) Yes, it is.

Madeleine Or maybe you began to think, maybe you began to *feel*: a life spent in children's clothes shops doesn't quite add up to a life.

Frances I didn't feel that. Why should I feel that?

Madeleine This way you can make experience into anything you want. Why not? Isn't that what a novelist does? A novelist re-orders. Isn't that the trick? Things acquire weight, they acquire meaning. Or they appear to. And isn't that what we want? Isn't that what everyone wants? That their lives should have meaning? Well? (*Madeleine waits for an answer.*) Oh, don't mistake me. If you think I'm envious, you're right. It would be nice, believe me, I see that. If life hadn't passed, if life hadn't just gone by . . . I would love nothing better. That would

34

be consolation. Re-order a few words, weave them into the pattern and suddenly there are no more bum notes. Suddenly there's melody. The time wasn't wasted after all.

Madeleine has sounded bitter. Frances speaks quietly.

Frances I don't feel I wasted my time. I was bringing up my children. Why is that time wasted?

Madeleine Oh, because the man you loved was with another woman. And because everything he said was a lie.

There's a silence while Frances decides how to respond to what Madeleine has said. Eventually she speaks.

Frances It's cold. Is your place always this cold?

Madeleine gets up to go over to the wardrobe to get Frances a cardigan.

Madeleine And now a memoir, you say?

Frances Yes.

Madeleine Not a novel?

Frances No.

Madeleine What, just simple, good-hearted prurience, is that the plan?

Frances No.

Madeleine What's it to be? The familiar story of a woman betrayed?

Frances I would hope not. I would hope more original than that.

Madeleine What then? Aren't Men Bastards?

Frances Hardly.

Madeleine That's a popular genre. Or: I Refuse to Be Defined. That's another genre. I Refuse to be Defined by the Man in My Life.

Frances Well, I do.

Madeleine Believe me, so do I. Always have. Plan to from now on. (*Madeleine holds out the cardigan.*) Here.

Frances Thank you. (*Frances puts it on and wraps it tightly round herself.*)

Madeleine And yes, if you're asking, if you really want to know, that's how the row came, as it happens.

Frances On the first night?

Madeleine Yes.

Frances The first night you met?

Madeleine Yes. 'I refuse to be defined.' On that very question.

Frances Tell me.

Madeleine 'Tell me' and what? 'Tell me' and next year I'll read it in a book?

Frances No.

There's a moment's silence. Frances is firm.

No. Just tell me.

Madeleine looks at her.

Madeleine I'd known him a few hours, I suppose. We'd been in church. We'd listened to Martin Luther King, and well . . . as we'd sat there – hard benches, long rows of straight hard benches – we'd thought, even at the time, even as we listened, we thought: 'This is something we'll remember for the rest of our lives.'

Frances Yes.

Madeleine And I have. (*Madeleine thinks a moment.*)
We went back to his motel. Made love. Then, in the
morning, 'I'll walk you back,' he said. 'Thanks, I don't
need it,' I said. 'I'll walk myself back.' (*Madeleine smiles
and says no more.*)

Frances So? Over that?

Madeleine Yes.

Frances You rowed?

Madeleine Yes. Over that. Like all the best rows,
blowing up out of a clear blue sky . . .

Frances Yes.

Madeleine And in themselves, deeply mysterious.
(*Madeleine shakes her head slightly.*) I said, 'Look, don't
walk me back. You don't have to walk me back like
you're doing me a favour.'

Frances You said that?

Madeleine Yes.

Frances What did he say?

Madeleine He said, 'I'm not doing you a favour. What is
this? I want to walk you back.'

   Madeleine stops. There is a silence.

Frances Then?

Madeleine I said, 'Apart from anything else, I'm some
years older than you, excuse me, I can walk through the
streets of Birmingham at dawn without a man's arm
round my shoulder. I don't need a man. Not for that.'
(*Madeleine stops again, thinking back.*) He was on the
bed. He was looking at me, that way he has. A bit lazy.

Veiled. He said, 'No really.' I said. 'No really nothing, except that we've just made love, we've made love twice over, and I knew the first time, not even the second. I knew. I can tell right now, because I foresee it, I can tell you right now: you will never love me enough. You do not love me enough.' (*Madeleine waits, silent.*)

Frances What did he answer?

Madeleine He said, 'Love you? We've only just met.' (*Madeleine turns and looks at Frances.*) And there you are. There it was . . .

Frances I see.

Madeleine Yes.

Frances Now I understand.

Madeleine Yes.

Frances Everything makes sense.

   There is a short silence.

I had no idea.

Madeleine A cheap hotel room in Alabama. There was a pale beige carpet. Pictures on the wall. Heliotrope and green. (*Madeleine points round, configuring the room anew.*) The bed to one side. Low. Opposite, the window. Brown curtains. A wardrobe, over there. And under the window, a pot plant. Also green. (*Madeleine smiles at the ridiculousness of the recall.*) Everything in my life leading to that moment . . .

Frances Yes.

Madeleine And then – sure as fuck – everything would then lead away.

Frances What happened?

Madeleine thinks a moment.

Madeleine I'd been around. I'd met some men. But never anything like this.

Frances No.

Madeleine It's true. (*Madeleine stands, defiant again.*) I will not be defined, I thought. I will not be defined by my need for this man.

Frances watches, not moving.

Frances What did you do?

Madeleine What do you think?

Frances I don't know. I'm not you.

Madeleine I went back to my boarding house.

Frances Alone?

Madeleine Yes. Alone. Of course. Back on the bus. Yes, I packed. I remember packing.

Frances You mean you left town?

Madeleine Yes. I left town. (*Madeleine thinks for a moment, then looks away.*) What does it matter? What difference did it make? It made no difference. Fifteen years later, I met him again.

There's a silence. Madeleine moves away to the window seat. Then Frances shakes her head, thinking over what she's just heard.

Frances We don't know anything, do we?

Madeleine No. Not much.

Frances We think we're being clever, but it's way beyond us. Most anyone can hope for is to avoid being stupid. (*Frances looks up.*) You see, I had no idea . . .

Madeleine Why would you?

Frances I mean, when was it? A few years ago, a few years ago, when I found out . . .

Madeleine Ah yes . . .

Frances . . . when I found out you existed.

There's a silence. Frances stops.

Madeleine Yes?

Frances He came home one evening. For years I'd had some impression, a sense, nothing more. That evening, I asked. For no reason. And for no reason, he told me. Oh, and he said, 'I knew her long before you.'

Frances looks to Madeleine for confirmation.

Madeleine It was true.

Frances looks away a moment.

Frances There was some funny thing that evening.

Madeleine What kind of thing?

Frances It was summer and we used to sit outside in the garden with a bottle of wine. He'd asked the vicar round. He'd met him in the street, he said, coming back from work. It was something he did. I'd noticed, he'd begun to do it quite often. I didn't quite get it.

Madeleine Well, no.

Frances It's not as if we'd ever been to church. Or knew the vicar, really. 'Vicar, what is the church's current thinking on original sin?' And as this poor man began to answer, Martin would signal, he'd start signalling to me . . .

Madeleine I can imagine.

Frances . . . sitting there, rolling his eyes, circling with his hand, as the vicar talked on. (*Frances imitates Martin's hand, revolving.*) 'The vicar's lonely,' he used to say afterwards, after the second bottle. Sometimes a third. 'If we don't invite him, nobody will.' But even before that evening I'd realised: it's not the vicar who's lonely.

Madeleine No.

Frances is regretful, remembering, before she goes on.

Frances 'The church's teaching on original sin,' he would say. 'You see, the thing that confuses me,' he would say – this was Martin, Martin would say, with a sort of relish, with a sense of fun, but also – I don't know, I think he also wanted to know. He would sit back in his chair, reach for his wine. 'Yours is such a *confusing* religion,' he would say . . .

Madeleine Yes.

Frances 'Man is born in sin, mired in sin, that's what your people say.'

Madeleine Well, they do.

Frances 'But what does that mean? Tell me what that actually means,' he would say. (*Frances shakes her head.*) I remember that particular evening, sitting, watching, my wine in my hand, thinking: he's talking to the vicar. One hour ago he told me something. I asked and he told me. And now, what? There he is, sweet, untidy, slightly fat, slightly bald, Martin Beale QC, radical lawyer, talking to the vicar, grinning at me, circling with his hand, smiling, as if he and I are in some sort of conspiracy, as if, of course, he and I *understand* one another . . . and I? I don't even know . . . I'm so lost, I'm so bereft, I'm thinking: what do I want? I don't even know what I want.

There is a pause.

'Are we condemned to struggle, vicar, do we have no choice? And, tell me, vicar, is it written? Are we foredoomed to fail?'

Madeleine just watches, saying nothing.

A couple of days later, as we're going upstairs. 'What was the orgy like?' I asked. 'Splendid,' he said. 'I wouldn't have missed it for the world.'

Madeleine grins at how characteristic this is.

I don't know . . . I really don't know. I was searching, I suppose, searching in him, for weeks, for months . . . like emptying an attic – what's that word? – *ransacking*, ransacking around inside Martin for a feeling. Looking all the time for a feeling.

Madeleine What feeling?

Frances Shame, I suppose.

Madeleine looks up sharply.

Madeleine And not finding it?

Suddenly Frances raises her voice, imitating Martin losing his temper.

Frances 'What do you want, then? Tell me,' he said. 'What do you want? What do you fucking well want? That we go on living this life? In a fucking walled garden in Blackheath? Frances, are you serious? Nothing to our lives except that?' (*Frances becomes quieter.*) 'And what if I'm hurt? What if it hurts, what you've told me?' He looked at me. 'Well then, you're hurt.'

There's a silence.

Days of thinking, 'Oh this is fine. I can handle this.' Then, 'Are you still seeing her?' 'Well, I am if that's OK with you.' 'Well, it's not OK with me.' 'Well it's what I'm going to do.' Then a long silence, a long, long silence, maybe thirty minutes or more. Maybe an hour. Then me getting up. 'Well if it's what you're going to do, why fucking ask? Why fucking ask?'

Madeleine smiles.

And he was funny, believe me, he was funny.

Madeleine I'm sure.

Frances I laughed.

Madeleine I'm sure.

Frances smiles now at a memory.

Frances Another evening I remember . . .

Madeleine Yes?

Frances This one sillier than any, problems with the plumbing, really, I mean, beyond parody –

Madeleine Beyond what you could write?

Frances Exactly.

Madeleine Yes.

Frances Beyond what I could invent – Martin in the cellar, stretched out under the boiler, me screaming, 'I want something back. I deserve something back.' Him saying, 'My aim is a fully functioning boiler.' (*Frances raises her voice again.*) 'I'm suffering and you're not!' 'Of course I'm suffering. You think I don't suffer?' 'May I see some evidence? *Please?*' (*Frances is still now, quiet.*) Finally, one night, very late, the worst night, up till then the worst night of all, his work papers all over the bed, I threw them out of the window. For hours I'd said the same thing. My child's blanket, my mantra, my refrain. 'I want something back, I deserve something back.' Him

43

pulling on his dressing gown. As he went out, turning. 'The world is not a court of law.' Just that. Nothing else. Then him down in the garden, picking up his papers from all over the lawn. (*Frances repeats the phrase, thoughtful.*) 'The world is not a court of law.' (*Frances is lost in her memories for a few moments.*) At five o'clock, me: 'What is it then?' He was sleeping beside me, as always, able to sleep. He woke. 'What is it?' 'Yes. If it's not a court of law?'

There is a silence.

What everyone wants, they say. Don't they say that? 'Love,' they say.

Madeleine Yes.

Frances The purpose of life: to find love.

Madeleine gets up, her beer glass empty.

Madeleine Are you hungry?

Frances Yes.

Madeleine We should eat. I'll get some takeaway.

Madeleine goes across to get her coat. Frances watches as she puts it on and then picks up her keys from the counter.

By the way – I'd heard it all. About the vicar coming round. I also knew about the boiler. And also the papers on the lawn. He told me. Just so you know.

Three

Night. The early hours. The neon is now dead. From the bedroom at the side, Madeleine comes into the room in her dressing gown. She walks gingerly across the room, expecting Frances to be asleep on the sofa, which is now made up as a bed. But Frances is sitting awake on the window seat, in borrowed pyjamas and dressing gown, looking out of the window. She turns at the sound of Madeleine coming into the room, but they can barely see each other.

Frances What are you doing?

Madeleine I've been lying awake. I realised I fancied some more korma.

Frances It's on the floor.

There is a litter of small silver tubs on the floor where they have eaten an improvised meal.

There's a poppadom somewhere if you haven't already trodden on it.

Madeleine sits down on the floor and resumes eating with a plastic fork from the foil containers.

Madeleine I talked to the man who owns the business. He and his family have travelled from Bangladesh to Ventnor. And now this is normal. We accept it as normal.

Frances Does it never occur to you to put things away? I could no more leave an Indian meal on the floor than leave a dead Indian there.

Madeleine I live alone. I can do what I like.

Madeleine is turned away from Frances, starting to eat.

Is the place unclean?

Frances No.

Madeleine Am I unclean?

Frances No. Spotless.

Madeleine Well then. (*Madeleine looks vindicated.*)

Frances You don't have a cigarette, by any chance?

Madeleine gets up silently and goes to the kitchen area.

Madeleine I didn't know you smoked.

Frances I smoke from time to time.

Madeleine As it happens, a man came round and left some.

Frances So you're not completely alone?

Without replying, Madeleine hands her the cigarettes and a box of matches.

Madeleine Here. Woodbines.

Frances Thank you.

Frances gets one out and smells it. Madeleine returns to her meal.

I last had a cigarette in the early seventies. Addictive, you see, as they allege. (*Frances lights a match.*) You don't mind? You don't mind if I smoke?

Madeleine Not in the slightest. Smoke all you like.

Frances I suppose your view is that we're only here once.

Madeleine Why, have they told you something different?

Frances inhales deeply.

How is it?

Frances Life-changing.

Madeleine There's a small scrap of okra which is doing the same job for me.

Frances Exhilarating, isn't it? (*Frances looks out of the window.*) At about three-fifteen a young couple went down the promenade . . .

Madeleine Ah yes. The regular stampede.

Frances smiles.

Frances I saw the porn cinema. I must say, I liked the sign.

Madeleine What sign?

Frances The one saying 'OAPs half-price before five p.m.'

Madeleine Oh, yes. Well, that's who we are. An island race, with rites and rituals in common. We all clean up before the cleaning lady comes.

Frances turns.

Frances I suppose one day it will change, won't it?

Madeleine Oh, sure.

Frances Even here.

Madeleine Oh, yes. The gentrifiers will come. One day. After all, they're everywhere else.

Frances They have to go *somewhere* next.

Madeleine They're smart.

Frances Like locusts.

47

Madeleine Exactly. I'm sure they can find their way to the hovercraft. (*Madeleine smiles to herself.*) The enemies of the bourgeois, isn't that what we called ourselves?

Frances You did. I didn't.

Madeleine And how did it turn out? The obituary of my generation. We left no loft unconverted. The revolutionary project: to leave the world a little more chic than we found it. Future historians will write: 'These are the people who took the world one notch up-market.'

Frances Not the whole world.

Madeleine No. Quite.

Frances You overlooked most of it.

Madeleine stops a moment.

Madeleine Well, there you are. We imagined we were protesting Vietnam. Looking back it seems like some of us were protesting their own future. A rare moment of prescience. A short carnival of revolt before the long luxury of self-improvement. Five years of protest. Thirty of acquiescence. Like allowing themselves a little scream before they jump in. Or a yell of 'No' when they mean 'Yes'. (*Madeleine mimics a question.*) 'What would Jesus do?'

There is a silence. Madeleine is eating and doesn't turn to look at Frances, who is watching her.

Madeleine And don't think because it's the middle of the night you're entitled to pity me.

Frances I must admit . . .

Madeleine I know . . .

Frances I did feel a slight weakening there.

Madeleine I sensed it. I could sense it . . .

Frances Just a moment . . .

Madeleine . . . even from behind.

Frances . . . that maybe you aren't a thoroughgoing bitch . . .

Madeleine Thank you.

Frances . . . and there's even something rather moving about you.

Madeleine doesn't react.

Madeleine That's right. I felt it. It came into the room. Like a smell.

Frances smiles, at ease.

Frances Don't worry. It's a mood. It'll pass.

Madeleine I'm your enemy. Don't lose sight of that.

Madeleine has said it casually and Frances seems relaxed when she speaks again.

Frances It's odd.

Madeleine What is?

Frances Oh, the feel of it. The smoke. It reminds me of school.

Madeleine Why school?

Frances My piano teacher used to lean across me, fag in hand, he used to lean across to reach a far note.

Madeleine Ah, yes.

Frances 'No, *this* one,' he'd say, carefully dropping ash in my lap. Then he'd brush my lap . . .

Madeleine Of course . . .

Frances . . . brush my lap with his hand. 'I'm sorry,' he'd say. 'I've spilt ash.'

Madeleine The devil. The dog. (*Madeleine smiles.*) Was this at a convent?

Frances How did you know?

Madeleine Oh . . . I suppose it just sounded like a sort of religious technique.

Frances Well you're right.

Madeleine Fingers flying, ash flying . . . (*Madeleine waves her hands appropriately.*) Clever, really. The things they come up with . . .

Frances The other day at my publishers' a man looked at me. He looked at me in a way I'd almost forgotten.

Madeleine The wreck of memory.

Frances Well, quite.

There's a moment's silence.

Madeleine Did he speak as well?

Frances He said, 'Would you like to have lunch?'

Madeleine Oh. Not an innovator, then, in his chosen field.

Frances No.

Madeleine Not a groundbreaker.

Frances 'Do I want to have lunch?' I wanted to say. 'What, you mean through a straw? What are you suggesting? A *date*? It's a little late, isn't it? Haven't we left it a little late for all that?'

Madeleine Why?

Frances doesn't answer.

Did you go? Aren't you what's called an attractive woman?

Frances If there was a brochure, you mean?

Madeleine Yes. In the brochure, you'd be what's called an attractive woman. Why shouldn't you date? You're free.

Again, Frances is silent, smoking.

Frances Another time, last year, someone at a party. Saying would I go in a cupboard with him?

Madeleine Really? (*Madeleine frowns.*) Any cupboard?

Frances No. On the landing outside.

Madeleine Did you?

Frances looks a second, then briefly nods an admission.

Frances As a matter of fact.

Madeleine Regret it?

Frances shakes her head.

Write about it?

Frances shakes her head again.

Well then, that's as near to a real experience as you're going to get. (*Madeleine reaches cheerfully for more food.*)

Frances You live like a student.

Madeleine Why not?

Frances Sure. If you can do it, why not?

Madeleine Get up in the night . . .

Frances Do you do this every night?

Madeleine I can. If I choose. And sleep all day. That's what I'm saying. Why not? We're free. (*Madeleine shrugs slightly.*) You learn the trick. To let go of time.

Frances puts out her cigarette, responding to what Madeleine has said.

Frances After Martin left, then the house was empty.

Madeleine Same thing.

Frances The children had gone. The house had been there for a purpose, it seemed. And now the purpose was served.

Madeleine Do you still live there?

Frances Yes. I'm there. (*Frances looks at her a moment.*) Outside in the street, the Range Rovers were still double-parked, disgorging children, belching children into the road, the mothers in their cotton jumpsuits, car keys in hand, sometimes the same cotton jumpsuits I had once worn – 'Can't stop,' 'Must rush,' 'Has Clarissa got her sandwiches?' – like an old film playing outside my window . . .

Madeleine has stopped eating to listen.

Frances Pacing the staircase. Pushing open the doors. The house became like the set for a play which was no longer performed . . . (*Frances turns and looks a moment at Madeleine.*) I would sit at my desk, notebook in hand: 'Can't call him Martin, must call him Michael. Mustn't be a lawyer. I'll put him in advertising.' Then one day I thought: 'What is this? What exactly is this layer I'm trying to add? This thin smear of fiction, this coating, this seal? What purpose does it serve?' I thought: 'What's interesting is what actually happened. That's what's arresting. What actually occurred. All right. So: I'm going to go after it, I'm going to pursue it, I'm going to find out everything. Just as it was. Exactly as it was.'

Madeleine pushes her paper plate aside.

Madeleine Seattle, you said?

Frances Yes.

Madeleine He went to Seattle?

Frances Yes. Because she was American.

Madeleine Of course.

Frances Came over.

Madeleine Of course.

Frances She was young. (*Frances smiles slightly.*) Oh yes, we'd heard a lot about youth in the previous few years. Even before she appeared. How wonderful the young were. How the young seemed to have something we didn't.

Madeleine Besides youth, you mean?

Frances A spirit, he said. An openness.

Madeleine Yes.

Frances 'Everything that was hard for us seems easy for them,' he said.

Madeleine Oh, I see . . .

Frances 'They're not hung up, they're not haunted,' he said.

Madeleine Did he say that?

Frances 'People say the young don't believe in anything any more. No ideals, no vision, they say. No how-it-should-be. But why is that bad? Why shouldn't that be an asset?' he said. 'Look at us,' he said . . .

Madeleine Well? (*Madeleine waits.*) Well?

Frances 'Nothing but vision. And where are we now?' (*Frances hesitates.*) One night, I asked: 'What, you mean with her you don't feel you're fucking a ghost?'

Madeleine turns, amused.

Madeleine My God, you really went for it, didn't you?

Frances Yes. In this case, I did.

Madeleine What did he say? What did he say to that?

Frances He said: 'I haven't fucked her.'

Madeleine I'm sorry?

Frances He said: 'Yes. I am going to go live with her – I will make my life with her – but, since you mention it, I haven't fucked her.'

Madeleine is taken aback. She stares at Frances, who looks back, level.

Madeleine Hey, hold on.

Frances That's it.

Madeleine Hold on a minute.

Frances smiles to herself.

Frances Ah, now you've come to life. Now I have your attention.

Madeleine Hadn't fucked her, eh?

Frances No. (*Frances waits a second, relishing the exact words.*) 'No,' he said . . .

Madeleine Go on.

Frances 'You see, this is different. I will sleep with her. I will. But only when I get to America.'

Madeleine sits a moment, awed.

Madeleine Wow! It is epic, isn't it?

Frances It is.

Madeleine I mean, you do have to admit. It is sort of epic.

Frances smiles, enjoying the moment.

What on earth is all this about?

Frances You tell me.

Madeleine What is he? A Founding Father? I mean, we're not talking *Mayflower* here, are we?

Frances Hardly.

Madeleine You're sure? They are planning to? They will, one day?

Frances Oh yes.

Madeleine What I'm saying is: she's not a Scientologist? This isn't arcane cult?

Frances Not as far as I know.

Madeleine shrugs, amused.

Madeleine Perhaps it's my grasp of colonial history, but it's my understanding that others have gone before. It's not as if it were a land crying out for Martin's seed, is it?

Frances pauses, for emphasis.

Frances 'If this one's to last,' he said. 'If this one's to be real . . .'

Madeleine is still looking in disbelief.

Madeleine I mean, it is something, isn't it?

Frances Yes.

Madeleine Self-denial arriving, as one might say, just a little late in Martin's life . . .

Frances Just a little.

Madeleine Something new in his life. New theory, is it? You mustn't despoil something valuable?

Frances Presumably.

Madeleine What is she? Too good to spoil? Too *rare* to spoil?

> *Frances spreads her hands as if to say Madeleine's guess is as good as hers.*

Mysterious contracts. Strange and arbitrary deadlines. This is normally called *religion*, isn't it? In most cultures, isn't that what it's called? Peculiar rules, and things done in the wrong order. Isn't this usually intended to satisfy some other Being, not present? Not the people with the actual desires?

Frances He didn't mention another Being.

Madeleine Well he wouldn't, would he?

> *There's a moment's silence.*

Madeleine Obviously, my dear, you and I acquiesced far too easily.

Frances So it appears.

Madeleine Know what? We sold ourselves cheap. Nobody told us. Are men still driven mad by denial?

Frances To be honest, I have to tell you, he seemed very happy.

Madeleine Did he?

Frances Very.

There's a sudden silence. Frances looks out of the window.

Frances Now, it turns out, he sends little notes to the children, invites them over . . .

Madeleine How *are* the children?

Frances Oh . . .

Madeleine Is she, so to speak – I mean, the question I'm asking: is she older than them?

Frances Not much. (*She looks at Madeleine a moment.*) Some sort of glass house they have, environmentally sound, so it appears, so the children say . . .

Madeleine They visited?

Frances Once.

Madeleine A glass house?

Frances Yes. On an estuary.

Madeleine Among forests?

Frances Well, yes.

Madeleine And does he have a pick-up truck and a wardrobe of brand new shirts?

Frances I'm sure.

Madeleine 'The red-check flannel this morning, darling? Or the green-check flannel?'

Frances smiles at the idea.

Frances 'Start again,' he said. 'I have that right, do I not? It's a human right. To start over.'

Madeleine stops, laying down her plastic knife and fork.

It has been strained. I mean, things had been strained for some time after I'd guessed. After I'd guessed about you.

Madeleine Things never recovered?

Frances hesitates.

Frances There were days I could tell, some days, somehow, I knew where he'd been. I'd ask him what he'd been doing that day. 'Oh, civil litigation,' he'd say.

Madeleine Really?

Frances Yes. I don't know why. It became a sort of code.

Madeleine Is that what I was?

Frances 'You're doing less criminal these days?' 'Yes,' he'd say, 'less criminal. More *civil*, for some reason,' he'd say.

They both smile.

We'd sit around in the evenings, you know. He'd be there. I'd be waiting. 'I'll make supper,' he'd say, getting up. And then, just to annoy him: 'So. How was she? How was she today?'

Madeleine is quiet, not moving.

'Why do you like her?' I'd say. 'What is it you like? Tell me, why do you need her? What do you need her for?'

Madeleine Did you say that?

Frances Dreading the answer, of course. Dreading what he would say.

There's a silence.

Madeleine What *did* he say?

Frances smiles that Madeleine has not been able to resist the question.

Frances 'Madeleine's different,' he'd say. 'One thing: she runs her own department,' he said, 'at the Museum. It's *her* department . . .'

Madeleine It certainly was.

Frances 'Islamic art. Ask anyone. She doesn't even speak to the boss . . .'

Madeleine I wouldn't. Why would I?

Frances 'She doesn't speak to anyone. She doesn't need to. She *needs* no one.' (*Frances stops a moment.*) Then he would look at me: 'Tell you what, tell you what I like about Madeleine. Madeleine? Finally, she doesn't give a damn. That's her secret. She doesn't need anyone to affirm her existence.'

There's a silence.

Madeleine I see. And what did you say to that?

Frances What could I say? I didn't know you, remember?

Madeleine No . . .

Frances I'd seen you one time only, remember? I'd met you once.

They both think back to their meeting, but then Frances smiles at a different memory.

But yes, actually, the next evening, since you ask, I did think of an answer . . .

Madeleine Did you?

Frances Yes. I came up with an answer.

Madeleine What did you say?

Frances We were in bed. I turned out the light. 'No needs, eh? Is that what you're saying? Is that what

59

you're describing? A woman without *needs*? Well, no wonder. She sounds like a fucking paragon, doesn't she?'

Madeleine Good for you.

Frances 'She sounds like a man's idea of heaven on wheels . . . ' 'Oh well,' says he. 'If you're just determined to be vulgar . . . '

They both laugh.

Madeleine He said that? What a prick.

Frances 'You know nothing,' he said. 'You understand nothing.'

There's a silence.

Madeleine What happened next?

Frances I turned on the light.

Madeleine Did you?

Frances Oh, sure. Just to annoy him. Lights on, lights off. Like the Nazis. I didn't watch all those war films for nothing.

Madeleine Well done.

Frances That's all I've got, remember? In my situation. The right to be incredibly annoying.

Madeleine You exercised that right?

Frances I did. To the full.

They both smile.

'Please reply to my question,' I said. 'Who exactly *is* this Madeleine? Getting up now – 'Excuse me, excuse me, but I have something to ask. I have something to ask and I want an answer.' Standing now at the end of the bed, turning on another light, then another. (*Frances suddenly raises her voice.*) 'Who is Madeleine? Who the hell is she? And why are we sharing? Tell me: why exactly am I sharing my husband with her?'

Madeleine smiles.

Madeleine Angry, was he?

Frances How did you know?

Madeleine I guessed.

There's a silence.

And what did he say?

Frances looks away.

Frances 'What's life become?' he said.

Madeleine Life?

Frances Our life.

Madeleine I see.

Frances pauses a second.

Frances 'Do you know what a family is?' he said. 'I'll tell you what it is. It's a unit of self-interest, an excuse for self-interest. That's why politicians love it,' he said. 'A self-motivating, self-perpetuating cartel, launched into the world to protect its own members, its only purpose to advance its own cause. Finally, a family is nothing but a crusade for itself. Ideal in theory, selfish in practice. What's a family? It's a trade union. It's an organised excuse for not caring about anyone else.' (*Frances stops, making her accusation direct to Madeleine.*) 'So?' I said. 'So?' (*Frances is now accusing Madeleine as if she were Martin, with the same anger.*) 'Madeleine,' he said, 'Madeleine stands outside. Madeleine's not complicit.'

Madeleine looks at her a moment.

Madeleine He said that? Those very words?

Frances I remember him saying: 'Where is Madeleine? Where is she now? Where is she, for instance, at this very moment? I can tell you,' he said. 'Madeleine goes out each evening, yes, nearly every evening – she goes out, after so many years . . . (*Frances suddenly raises her voice.*) 'The end of the system!' he said . . .

Madeleine I see . . .

Frances 'The end of the system! Whatever that may mean – whatever that may be – that's what she's working for – that's what she says she's working for, at God knows what age, there she is, day in, day out, working for something called the end of the system!'

Madeleine Well?

Frances 'She's still campaigning, yes, Madeleine's campaigning when the world tells her there's no reason, when the world says there's no cause. When the whole world tells her there's no fucking chance in the world of anything changing, *nothing* changing – when we all know nothing will change –' (*Frances has inhabited Martin's anger now as if it were her own.*) 'What is that?' he said. 'What do we call that? What is the word for being alone and not giving in? For being the same person you were thirty years ago? Forty? What is the word for that?'

> *There is a silence. Frances is still waiting as if she expects a response.*

Madeleine Did he say more?

Frances 'Not to need – not even to need – Madeleine doesn't expect the consolations of history. This woman expects nothing. She asks for nothing. No other satisfaction but the satisfaction of believing she may one day be right.

There is a silence, Madeleine waiting for her to go on.

'What do we call that? What is the name for that?'

Madeleine looks down.

Madeleine I see.

Frances Yes.

Madeleine Well, of course . . .

Frances Yes.

Madeleine Well . . .

Frances Yes.

Madeleine There we are.

Frances is nodding, the anger now her own and deep inside in her.

Frances And this is a different *kind* of row, believe me . . .

Madeleine I'm sure . . .

Frances This is a different *level* of row . . .

Madeleine It would be.

Frances This row isn't like papers on the lawn. Oh no, this isn't one he's going to go back and tell his girlfriend about.

Madeleine No . . .

Frances He's not proud of this one. This, believe me, is like arguing on top of Everest. And me, I'm fighting for air. I'm gasping. (*Frances raises her voice, threatening.*) 'Excuse me,' I say, 'forgive me if I'm mistaken, but something here makes me feel, I detect somehow: a comparison is being made.' He shouts. 'Too right,' he says. 'Too fucking right.' (*Frances is suddenly quiet.*)

63

Then: 'I need her strength,' he says. 'I need that strength.'

There is a silence. Madeleine impulsively gathers up the empty cartons and takes them into the kitchen. Frances reaches for another cigarette.

Madeleine Did he say that?

Frances I'm at the end of the bed. I'm standing at the end of the bed.

Madeleine Where's he?

Frances In the bed.

Madeleine I see.

Frances He's still in the bed. Yeah. In fact, he's lighting a cigarette. So Martin. Not thinking about it. Just doing it. (*Frances puts a cigarette in her mouth.*) Me, I'm standing there, I'm shaking. 'You're looking for a word, you say. You say you want a particular word. I think I know the word you're looking for.' 'Do you?' he says. I say: 'The word is "heroic", isn't it? Isn't that the word? "Heroic"?'

Madeleine is quite still.

He looks at me. 'It may very well be.'

Frances lights the cigarette. Madeleine is uneasy, upset.

Madeleine Frances . . .

Frances All right, very good, let's go on from there, I say, let's just move right on down, shall we? I mean, moving right on, I think we can guess what's *not* heroic, can't we?

Madeleine I'm sure you can.

Frances I don't think that's hard to guess.

Madeleine No.

Frances It isn't, is it? Bringing up children. Caring for your family. Being a wife. That's not heroic, is it? In fact, about as heroic as shifting garbage . . .

Madeleine Sure . . .

Frances . . . disposing of garbage . . .

Madeleine is close, watching now.

'Excuse me,' I say, 'but aren't we talking about something called balance here? Isn't there something called *balance?*

Frances drags at her cigarette fiercely, fighting the tears in her eyes.

'Wouldn't you say, wouldn't you feel, Martin, that most people live in a mess? Most people we know live in a sort of mess?'

Madeleine Sure.

Frances That's what they feel. As you would say, just getting up in the morning, barely knowing why, barely knowing what they're trying to do except love their children, be loyal to their friends . . . I don't know . . . maybe be loyal to their children, love their friends.

Madeleine Yes.

Frances That's how they live. Not convinced of anything. Not sure.

Madeleine Of course.

Frances No plan. No 'view'. Just trying to express themselves – I don't know – most people express themselves by simply trying to be kind. Wouldn't you say?

Madeleine Of course.

Frances By small daily acts of kindness.

Madeleine waits.

Madeleine Well?

But Frances doesn't go on.

Madeleine Well?

Frances And, yes, all right, I admit, it may very well be, most of those acts are directed at people who are closest to them. So? Does that make them wrong? (*Frances stops again, as if expecting an answer.*) These acts still count for something? They do count for something, don't they?

Madeleine Of course!

Frances Don't they? If that's how we live? If that's the way most of us know best *how* to live?

Madeleine Of course!

Frances Just wanting to help. Wanting to be of some use. That has some value, doesn't it? That still counts, doesn't it?

Madeleine Of course. What are you saying? Of course! (*Madeleine is becoming irritated by Frances's inquisition.*)

Frances 'All right, very well, explain to me, then. This woman, you say, this woman you love – she's meant to be different. Madeleine is different. Why? Because she lives to a plan. She has a "view". She got her view – didn't she? – when did she get it? In the sixties, was it? Was it in the sixties, she got her idea – is that right? – her practical idea of how she would like the world to change? And, what, she's stuck to that idea, has she? What, stuck to it, stuck to it stubbornly through the years in the face of all evidence to the contrary?'

Madeleine It wasn't just in the sixties.

Frances Really?

Madeleine No.

Frances looks at her disbelievingly.

It isn't just the sixties.

Frances 'And we admire her for that, do we? That's what we admire her for? That makes her strong, does it? She's a strong person, is she, because a fantasy sustains her? The past sustains her?'

Now it is Madeleine's turn to look unforgiving.

Madeleine Did you really say that? What point were you making?

Frances You know what point.

Madeleine And?

Frances says nothing.

Well?

Frances I'm just saying.

Madeleine What business was it of yours?

Frances I'm not saying it's my business. I'm just explaining.

Madeleine My God, you think *I* live in the past!

Frances I think you do.

Madeleine If it's living in the past: if that's the crime, if *that's* the accusation . . .

Frances There's no crime. There's no accusation. (*Frances is suddenly level, just looking Madeleine in the eye.*)

Madeleine Go on.

Frances So. He looks at me. He smiles. 'You can talk all you like,' he says . . .

Madeleine Too right.

Frances 'You can say what you like. You can't alter the facts. It's not her ideas. It's not because of what she believes that I'm with her.'

Madeleine No?

Frances 'That's not why I'm with her.'

Madeleine hesitates a moment.

Madeleine Why, then? Why was he with me?

There's a silence. Frances smokes her cigarette, then looks at Madeleine, waiting for her to speak.

Frances You say.

Madeleine looks at her as if the idea were ridiculous.

Frances No, really. You tell me for once.

Madeleine Are you serious?

Frances Of course.

Madeleine You want me to tell you?

Frances Of course.

Madeleine Why Martin loved me? (*Madeleine smiles and shakes her head.*) I don't think so. No. No, I don't think so.

Frances Why not?

Madeleine I would have thought for the obvious reason.

Frances Oh yes? What reason is that?

Madeleine Oh Frances, please! (*Madeleine has suddenly lost patience.*) What do you think? Do you think I'm completely naive?

Frances Why not? (*Frances is alive now, not giving up.*) No, really I'm interested. You've told me a lot of things . . .

Madeleine Have I? Do you think I have, really?

Frances Of course. How you met. How you fell in love. Why did you tell me if you didn't want me to know? Now suddenly – I don't know – you want to hold out on me. Why? What's the problem?

Frances is smiling as Madeleine looks at her distrustfully.

Tell me: am I getting too close?

Frances has asked this last question with sudden silky confidence. Madeleine looks at her, decisive now, resolving to take her on.

Madeleine All right, no doubt in your view I've done a lot of stupid things in my life . . .

Frances I didn't say that.

Madeleine That's what you meant.

Frances That's not what I said.

Madeleine Oh yes. in your view I've wasted a lot of time – going to meetings, attending meetings . . . (*Madeleine stops a moment, focusing on Frances.*) But in all that there's one thing I've never done, believe me.

Frances What's that?

Madeleine Let myself be used. I won't be used.

Frances Used?

There is a sudden silence.

You think I'm using you?

Madeleine looks at her as if it were self-evident.

Madeleine You walk through my door, is that right? You come barging through my door, and you flash your badge. Somehow that entitles you, does it? You're allowed into my apartment, are you? You have a licence, do you? 'Let me through, I'm a writer'?

Frances Of course not.

Madeleine I haven't seen it yet. What does it say? What does it say on your warrant? 'In pursuit of emotional inquiries'?

Frances Very funny.

Madeleine Who are you? Kojak?

Frances I thought you didn't have a television.

Madeleine I don't have a television *now*.

Frances looks at her resentfully.

'Who loves ya, baby?'

Frances Oh yes, very good . . .

Madeleine All right, it's true, I don't get out much, I'm pretty out of touch, I admit it, but even I know a blocked novelist when I see one. (*Madeleine has spat the last accusation out with sudden, unexpected malice.*)

Frances That isn't fair. How dare you? That isn't fair.

Madeleine Isn't it? (*Now Madeleine squares confidently up to her from across the room.*) This is normal, is it? I mean, this is an everyday situation for you, is it?

Frances No.

Madeleine This happens often, does it?

Frances No.

70

Madeleine Frances, what am I to you? Copy?

Frances No.

Madeleine What am I? A source? Am I being pumped? Am I being squeezed?

Frances No.

Madeleine What then? Explain.

Frances shifts, defensive.

Frances We're talking. That's all. It's the middle of the night. And we're talking. There are things . . . there are things I need to know.

Madeleine stands, waiting for more.

Madeleine Is that all?

Frances Don't you want to talk? Even you. You can't be alone all the time. Isn't it a human instinct? To share?

Madeleine Sure. It's human to talk.

Frances Well then . . .

Madeleine But is it human to write it down afterwards?

Frances puts up her hands as if in defence, but Madeleine is turning, her attack ignited.

Frances All right . . .

Madeleine And so explain, what is this new fashion exactly? Tell me. If it's not a novel.

Frances It's not.

Madeleine If it's 'real life'. What is this new genre?

Frances I said.

Madeleine Yes, but forgive me: didn't people use to wait until their subjects were *dead*? Wasn't that the procedure?

Die, *then* write? Now, what, we're all so impatient, are we . . .

Frances No . . .

Madeleine . . . we're all so desperate? What's the plan? We all bury the body while it's still living?

Frances That's not what I'm doing.

Madeleine Isn't it? (*Now Madeleine is coming out from the kitchen area, as if struck by a new thought.*) In fact, hold on. Can I ask a question? Do you mind? Can I just ask something now?

Frances Please. Ask what you like.

Madeleine Very well then. What the hell are you doing here? (*Madeleine begins to nod.*) I mean just that. That is my question.

Frances What am I doing here?

Madeleine That is what I'm asking. Yes.

Frances You know what I'm doing here.

Madeleine No, actually I don't. Do you know? Ever since you arrived. I don't. (*Madeleine turns, ignoring her.*) Four o'clock in the morning. There's a woman in my living room. I seem to have forgotten: did she just drop by for a curry?

Frances No. I didn't drop by for a curry.

Madeleine turns and looks at Frances.

Madeleine And something else, something else I'm not getting: what exactly is this famous book meant to be?

Frances What is it?

Madeleine Yes.

Frances I told you. I already explained.

Madeleine Did you?

Frances I told you. It's something new. It's . . .

Madeleine What? What is it exactly?

Madeleine looks at her, unrelenting. Frances gets up impulsively and walks across the room. There is a silence.

Frances My God, you can be tough. I came in distress. Isn't that obvious? That's why I came.

Madeleine Distress with a strategy or distress without? (*Madeleine waits.*) Well?

Now Frances smiles at the absurdity of her situation.

Frances It's that word. I can't even say it. The word itself is stupid.

Madeleine What word?

Frances The word Americans use. When Americans want things to be over.

Madeleine Oh. Closure.

Frances Yes.

Madeleine They ask for closure.

Frances Just that. Some sort of end to the pain.

Madeleine is nodding slightly as if taking things in.

Madeleine Well, I must say . . .

Frances Yes . . .

Madeleine . . . if that's what you want . . .

Frances It is.

Madeleine . . . if it's closure you want, you've chosen a rare way of getting it.

Frances looks at Madeleine a moment.

73

No, I mean, really. Closure! What, preceded by serialisation in a Sunday paper?

Frances No!

Madeleine What's the plan? Smother the pain with publicity?

Frances looks away, but Madeleine is going on.

And the form?

Frances I'm sorry?

Madeleine The form of the book?

Frances What about it?

Madeleine I'm asking. What form this book is in. What shape.

Frances looks bewildered.

Frances Currently?

Madeleine Yes.

Frances In the form of notes.

Madeleine Notes? And chapters? Are there actual written chapters?

Frances looks at her resentfully, her silence its own answer.

You want to come to my flat, let's face it, a book is a convenient excuse. It's a perfect excuse. (*Madeleine turns and looks at her again.*) Does the book exist?

The room has become very quiet, the two women still. From Frances there is a silent concession, which resolves the conversation, Madeleine nods at Frances's implicit admission.

It's in your mind, isn't it?

Frances Yes.

Madeleine And in mine.

There is a silence. Madeleine seems satisfied, and at last relaxes.

So. Do you want to go to bed? Do you want to go back to bed?

Frances In a moment. Soon. Thank you.

Madeleine Be my guest. (*Madeleine smiles now as if at some unspoken thought.*) I mean, I'm not a writer, but, if you want my opinion, this is the best scene you've got.

Frances What is?

Madeleine This. *This*. (*Madeleine gestures around her.*)

Frances Oh.

Madeleine Here. Now.

Frances Ah yes.

Madeleine In this room. It's a powerful atmosphere.

Frances Yes.

Madeleine Can you describe that atmosphere?

Frances doesn't answer.

You visit the girlfriend. She lives on the Isle of Wight. You fall asleep. You fall asleep on the sofa. Hey, it's a good scene. That's a very good scene. You wake up. You've missed the boat . . . (*Madeleine nods as if to say 'Not bad.'*) Well, it's your book, Frances, you must do what you think best, but if you want my opinion: you need this scene. You need it. Otherwise, what have you got? Not much. Twenty-five years of deceit. I'm being honest. That's not much. Man betrays woman on daily basis for a quarter of a century. I mean, it's not exactly

War and Peace, is it? It's not *Les Misérables.* Fact is, if
you don't do this scene – I'm being frank with you – if
you don't do the scene on the Isle of Wight, then I don't
think you have a climax. Without this particular scene,
without telling how you came to my door, your story has
no climax. And without a climax, without a real climax,
well . . . forgive me, to get away with that, you'd have to
be what they call a literary writer. That's my impression.
A literary writer is allowed to write a book with no
shape. But not a popular writer. Not one as popular as
you are. (*Madeleine smiles.*) I suppose you could say,
just to be brutal for a moment, I'm just talking in sheer
commercial terms now: unless the wife confronts the
girlfriend, I honestly don't feel you've got a book at all.
(*Madeleine looks her a moment in the eye, then turns.*)
I'm going to bed. Is there anything you need?

Frances Nothing.

> *Madeleine heads for the door, but stops before she
> goes out.*

Madeleine What I don't understand, by the way: I'm
what's called a difficult person, and you're what's called
a nice person. But, as you recount it, you're planning to
do something I would never even consider. Can you
explain?

> *Frances looks at her a moment.*

Frances I would like another cigarette.

Madeleine Take the pack. Goodnight.

> *Madeleine goes out. Frances walks across to the
> window seat and takes out another cigarette. She
> lights it.*

Four

Morning. There is bright sunshine outside. The temporary bed has been cleared away. Madeleine is sitting at a small table, on which there is an enamel coffee pot, hot milk, and two French bowls for drinking coffee. She is in jeans and a jumper and seems in remarkably good spirits. She is opening her mail. Frances comes from the bathroom, dressed again for the world and freshly made up. She walks across to order her things for her imminent departure. Madeleine holds a typed letter above her head.

Madeleine Oh look, it's started.

Frances What?

Madeleine I've had a letter.

Frances What sort of letter?

Frances comes across to pour herself coffee from the piping hot pot, as Madeleine reads.

Madeleine 'Our client, Mr P, a well-known and highly respected merchant banker, has approached us with a view to acquiring property in this area. This is a genuine inquiry.' That's in capital letters. What do you think?

Frances Obvious hoax.

Madeleine I thought so too. What are they, burglars? (*Madeleine resumes reading.*) 'Mr P is willing to pay a top price to be on the seafront.' It all sounds vaguely indecent. Do you think Mr P's in some kind of scene with Miss Q?

Frances It's what you said. There's nowhere left.

Frances smiles easily and goes to the kitchen area to search for sugar. Madeleine puts the letter aside.

Madeleine No question, it's true what they say.

Frances What is?

Madeleine In every country in the world. Think about it. Florida. The Côte d'Azur. The rubbish always falls to the bottom.

Frances smiles, returning with some sugar lumps.

Bavaria. Jesus! Fruitcakes fly south.

Frances sits at the other side of the table.

Frances Then why did you head this way?

Madeleine Why do you think?

Frances I don't know.

Madeleine For the obvious reason. I woke up one morning, I was sixty. I don't have a great deal of time left. I was looking for a place where it would go as slowly as possible. I mean, didn't the night seem long?

Frances Interminable.

Madeleine There you are, you see. That's the Isle of Wight. More bangs for your buck.

Frances hesitates.

Frances It wasn't . . .

Madeleine What?

Frances No . . . you didn't come here for another reason? Somehow I assumed you might have come to escape.

Madeleine Escape?

Frances Well, I just wondered.

Madeleine waits a moment, sorrowful.

Madeleine Frances, can I just ask you something?

Frances Of course.

Madeleine Do you think at this moment – no, not literally at this moment, I mean in eight hours' time – do you think a man will get up in a glass house on an estuary in Seattle and sit at breakfast talking about us?

Frances No.

Madeleine Good. Then shall we not talk about him? Shall we just have a pleasant cup of coffee? It's more dignified.

They both smile.

Frances As you wish.

Madeleine I can't believe it hasn't occurred to you: apart from anything, it's boring living in the past.

Frances Tell me about it.

Madeleine Because the worst thing about living in the past, I'd have thought, is that you always know what's going to happen.

Frances Well, I do.

Madeleine He's going to leave you.

Frances Quite.

Madeleine He always leaves you. He never doesn't. (*Madeleine shrugs at the inevitability.*) There it is. He runs off with a milk-fed American with a magnificent figure and finds God.

Frances How do you know?

Madeleine Because – just guessing – but that's generally the form God takes when He presents himself to middle-aged lawyers. And middle-aged is putting it kindly. Aren't I right? (*Madeleine waves a hand, definitive.*) Forget it. Forget him.

Frances You seem cheerful this morning.

Madeleine I am. I am cheerful. Why shouldn't I be cheerful? The boats are running.

Frances Thank you.

Madeleine Not at all. (*Madeleine looks pleased.*)

Frances What will you do?

Madeleine When?

Frances Today. What will you do when I leave?

Madeleine What will I do? I'll close that door and go back to my work.

Frances Is that what you do? Every day?

Madeleine looks warmly at Frances a moment across the small table.

Madeleine There's satisfaction, isn't there? Don't you find?

Frances Of course.

Madeleine As you get older?

Frances Of course.

Madeleine smiles to herself.

Madeleine After all, you can hardly be working for any ulterior motive. What motive? Ambition? Hardly. To make your mark? Your mark is made. For the little it meant. Self-advancement? Advance to where? No. You do the work only because you need to.

Frances What do you actually do?

Madeleine Provenance. My field is provenance. I seek the origin of things. Unlike you. I discover. Then I describe. You can only draw conclusions, you can only theorise when you have the whole picture. And who has the whole picture? (*Madeleine shakes her head, replying to her own question.*) People say scholarship is dry. It never seems dry to me, because it's always adding. Scholarship comes along and says, 'And also this.' 'Here's another thing.' There's peace in that. There's pleasure. (*Madeleine is silent a moment longer, then breaks her own mood.*)

Frances Yes.

Madeleine I'm happy among books. Books are easier than people. You can put a book down and you don't hurt its feelings.

Frances Well, that's true.

Madeleine The back-breaking effort of tact is not required. Thank God. No need for restraint.

Frances And when did you ever practise restraint?

Madeleine Well, it's not been high on my list of virtues.

Frances No.

Madeleine It's never come top.

Frances No? What did? What did come top?

Madeleine smiles to herself and reaches for more coffee.

Madeleine You don't give up, do you?

Frances Me? No.

Madeleine Still asking questions . . .

Frances . . . oh yes . . .

Madeleine Even at this late stage. Even as the ship's engine is turning. Even as the hovercraft hovers.

Frances does not look away.

Frances Well?

Madeleine I'll say this for you: you do bounce back, don't you?

Frances I've always bounced back.

Madeleine I'm sure.

Frances So?

Madeleine looks at her across the table, as if considering her.

Frances What? What are you thinking?

Madeleine What I've been thinking all night.

Frances What's that?

Madeleine How someone who has so much courage could have so little confidence. (*Madeleine waits a moment, then nods.*) Yes. Just that.

Madeleine gets up and takes her bowl to the sink. Frances does not move.

I'll walk you down the road.

Frances Thank you.

Madeleine I'll get my coat.

Madeleine heads for the bedroom door, but before she gets there, Frances speaks.

Frances Madeleine . . .

Madeleine Yes?

Frances I've also been thinking. The book. The book I was going to write.

Madeleine Ah. You've decided?

Frances Yes. (*Frances hesitates a second.*) I'm no longer writing it.

Madeleine waits a moment, giving nothing away.

Madeleine You won't write it now, or you won't write it ever?

Frances Ever.

Madeleine shows no reaction at all, just remains standing by the bedroom door.

Frances It's not going to be written.

Madeleine Well, good.

Madeleine turns and goes out. Frances stands alone. She looks across to Madeleine's desk where the computer is already on for the day's work. Frances goes across to look, but then sees a small, framed photograph hidden away at the back of the desk. She picks it up, curious, and stands looking at it. Madeleine returns.

Frances This photo . . .

Madeleine Yes?

Frances What is it? What is this photo?

Madeleine What does it look like?

Frances Two people in America, absurdly young.

Madeleine Yes. (*Madeleine is stilled as if tensing herself for what will happen next.*) Then that's what it is.

Frances turns, still holding the photograph.

Frances Will you tell me? Please?

Madeleine Frances . . .

Frances Will you tell me what happened?

Madeleine hesitates, not answering.

Completing the picture, you said . . .

Madeleine No . . .

Frances That's what you said.

Madeleine I didn't say completing. Adding.

Frances Yes.

Madeleine Adding to the picture, I said.

Frances looks at her a moment.

Frances You see, when I leave . . . when I leave this island, it's clear, we won't meet again.

Madeleine It doesn't seem likely.

Frances We'll never meet again.

Madeleine We agree.

Frances shakes her head slightly.

Frances So everything you've said . . .

Madeleine Yes . . .

Frances I'll remember. The words you used, the phrases.

Madeleine I'm sure.

Frances What you gave me. What you withheld. 'What did this mean?' 'Why did she put it like that?'

Madeleine Yes . . .

Frances Even the smell of the room, how the sea sounded this morning as I was lying awake . . .

Madeleine still stands, considering.

You've always had the advantage, remember? Because you always knew I existed. Isn't it easier? Isn't it always easier to live when you know?

There's a silence. Madeleine moves across the room. Frances watches.

Madeleine It was in the spring. If that's going to help.

Frances I think it's going to help.

Madeleine If it's what you want to hear.

Frances I don't know. (*Frances shakes her head.*) I don't know what I want to hear. Try me.

Madeleine What?

Frances Anything.

Madeleine sits down on a hard chair.

Madeleine I think what you need to know is: it was an early day in spring.

Frances When? When was this?

Madeleine Oh. The late seventies. I suppose. Was it? Does it matter?

Frances You must know.

Madeleine frowns, almost vague.

Madeleine Yes. It has to be the seventies. It could only be. Me back in England, qualified and on my way.

Frances Well set, as they say.

Madeleine Yes. 'Well set.' (*Madeleine thinks a moment.*)
A degree, a flat, a job at the Museum. Content and
discontent. The characteristic state of the aspirant
middle class – lucky and unlucky, feeling permanent and
also . . . I don't know . . . on shifting sand. 'This can't
last.' The feeling of the time: 'Something will happen,
this can't go on.' Every evening, a circle of friends. The
company of like-minded people. Talk of revolution, and
everyone believing in the power of ideas. (*Madeleine
stops a moment.*) One day, coming out of a side door
in Bloomsbury a voice behind me. 'Madeleine, it's you.'
(*Madeleine smiles to herself.*) He was wearing a mac.
Some strange – I don't know, cape-like thing. Older, of
course. The hair thinning. No longer in jeans. But still –
the same air of amusement, the sense of the unspoken
joke. (*Madeleine turns and looks at Frances.*) There was
a case, he said . . .

Frances That's right . . .

Madeleine Concerning the Museum.

Frances That's right.

Madeleine He'd been in the Museum. He didn't know
I worked there, he said. (*Madeleine stops a second,
recalling.*) Well. Close to the Museum there's a sort of
colonnade, it's hard to describe –

Frances Sicilian Avenue –

Madeleine Yes. A mock Italian arcade. He said there was
a place to eat. With mock-Italian food. I said, 'Thank you
but I've eaten already.' There was a silence. I remember
saying, 'It's been nice to see you. And now I must go.'
(*Madeleine shrugs slightly.*) So there it was. He was
holding an umbrella, he was looking at me and I knew
what he was thinking. 'I didn't take you for a liar.' Or
rather, 'If you're going to lie, lie better. Lie well.'

Frances Yes.

Madeleine He still said nothing. I said, 'I've got a little time. If you're going to eat, I'll just watch.' (*Madeleine smiles, completely absorbed.*) So we walked along the street, saying nothing. He ordered Pasta Putanesca and distressed salad. 'I want my salad distressed,' he said. When the spaghetti came he asked for a second fork and I ate the lot. He ate nothing. He never touched his fork.

Frances is listening intently now, taking in every word.

He asked me what I'd been doing. I told him I'd gone to study at Berkeley. I'd stayed in the States for five years. I'd not left. 'You?' 'Law,' he said. 'Marriage.' (*Madeleine looks at Frances, amused.*) It was funny, there was something, there was something in the way he said it: 'Law. Marriage.' Like the doors of a vault, closing. I told him I had friends who'd done some strange things, wild things – they'd joined bands, taken drugs, I knew one boy blew himself up, burnt himself to death – but nobody I knew had married. I looked at him. 'You must know something I don't.' (*Madeleine has become very quiet.*) It was odd. There was thunder, and so much rain that we couldn't leave. At least that's what we said. My hand was on the table. I knew it was there, but I didn't move it. (*Madeleine is quite still.*) He didn't even try to explain. Didn't have to. 'There was a tone of voice, wasn't there?' he said. 'When we were in America. At that moment of hope, in America. It's a voice which moves me,' he said. 'I've not heard it again.' (*Madeleine stops again for a second.*) Then he said: 'I'm an advocate now. That's what I do. I put a case.' (*Madeleine turns and looks at Frances as if this last, flat statement summed everything up.*) The sun came out and we walked for a while. I remember him saying: 'Don't you have to go back?' (*Madeleine shrugs.*) You could say, on the one hand, nothing had changed. Nothing had

87

changed from fifteen years earlier. We were the same people. 'I'd like to see the river,' I said. There's a bit on Waterloo Bridge, do you know?

Frances Yes.

Madeleine Do you know it?

Frances Yes.

Madeleine You can stand on Waterloo Bridge. (*Madeleine pauses a second.*) 'Why did you leave?' he said. 'Why did you leave me that day?' (*Madeleine smiles at the question.*) It was one of those evenings, the sun came out – I don't remember the order of things. In fact, Martin always said – you know, he said: 'Don't trust an accurate witness . . .'

Frances Yes . . .

Madeleine In court, he said, when you're asking questions in court, the person who claims to remember exactly, *exactly* what happened . . .

Frances He said that . . .

Madeleine . . . yes . . . well, juries don't like them . . .

Frances No . . .

Madeleine . . . juries don't trust them. They prefer a witness who says, 'I think that's what happened, but I may be wrong.' (*Madeleine smiles at the oddness of it.*) So you see, we were there . . .

Frances Yes . . .

Madeleine We sat by the river. He didn't want to go back. Over and over, he said to me, 'Why did you leave?' Then he said, 'If you hadn't left that morning . . .' And I said, 'What? What exactly? If I hadn't left?' He smiled. He just said, 'None of this would have happened.'

(*Madeleine smiles at Frances.*) And, honestly, I don't think I even asked what he meant by 'all this'.

Frances He meant me.

Madeleine No. Not you. Not really. (*Madeleine frowns, as if this were too crude.*) I think . . . I think he meant something vaguer . . .

Frances I know what he meant.

Madeleine Something larger.

Frances Of course. Do you think I don't know? I know! (*Frances is suddenly angered and can't stop herself.*) 'Things might have been different!' That's what he was saying. It makes me angry. Because what does it mean? What does it mean to say things might have been different? Different how? That you wouldn't have to grow up? That you wouldn't one day have had to grow up? Is that what he's saying? He could have stayed young? It's childish! Who stays young?

Frances has asked this last question with real bitterness, but Madeleine just looks down.

Madeleine Anyway . . .

Frances I know . . .

Madeleine All right . . .

Frances I'm sorry. I'll be quiet. I'll listen.

Madeleine Whatever.

There's a silence.

Madeleine Let's just say, I knew why he was upset.

Frances He was blaming you.

Madeleine No, that's not fair to him.

Frances Wasn't he?

89

Madeleine There was no blame. Just . . . bewilderment. It was something he couldn't understand. He couldn't. 'Why did you run? Why did you leave me?' (*Madeleine smiles at the repetition.*) 'If you hadn't left me that morning in America . . .' (*Madeleine leaves the thought suspended a moment, then is seen to remember the scene.*) There's a sort of bend in the river, I can't tell you . . .

Frances Yes . . .

Madeleine There's a kind of light when evening comes down . . . It's funny, people always use that word, 'backdrop'. They always used it in novels. Do you?

Frances I have done.

Madeleine 'The majestic backdrop,' they say. As if nature somehow whips out something suitable, gives you suitable splendour at the right moment. As if nature knew.

Frances is intent again now.

I said, 'Why do you think I left you?' He said, 'I have no idea.' So I told him. I said, 'I was frightened.' He said, 'Frightened of what?' (*Madeleine turns and looks at Frances.*) I said I was frightened it might turn out less than I hoped.

They are both now completely still.

Just that. Nothing else. Only. Wanting everything and fearing I'd only get something. That was the reason.

There is a silence. Now Madeleine is deeply affected by her own story.

Then he said: 'Is that still how you feel?' (*Madeleine shakes her head as if no answer were possible.*) It's silly, isn't it? So silly. Anyone else in the world would have said, 'Take what you can.' Why not? Take it. That's what

90

everyone does. That's where we live. All of us. In the kingdom of the feelings. 'I want this. I'll get it. I'll have it.' Why not? I don't know why I'd once thought I was some sort of exception. Some stupid girl in America. 'If it's not perfect I'm not going to take it.' (*Madeleine smiles at her own stupidity.*) Who did I think I was?

    There is a silence.

And what was the price? Not having him.

Frances Yes.

Madeleine Why was that wonderful? What was so great about that? (*Madeleine, the question unanswerable.*) So. This time, we walked by the river. Found a hotel room. Another view of the Thames. He rang you, said he'd be late. That night, I remember walking back home. By midnight, Covent Garden deserted. The rain on the streets. Thinking: so this is it. Fifteen years on. This is what it feels like. I've settled for less. He won't be my life. He'll be the commentary.

    There's a silence.

And I suppose we went on from there. (*Now Madeleine smiles at Frances.*) I only saw you once, remember?

Frances Of course.

Madeleine You came to the Museum.

Frances A fund-raiser.

Madeleine Yes. A few years later, I guess. You had brilliant-blue shoes. Just like the Queen in your dream. You were acting – oh . . . intense interest and warmth. Oh so interested in everything everyone said. Looking round the room. His hand on your back. (*Madeleine smiles.*) He introduced us.

Frances Yes.

Madeleine You had a sausage on a toothpick.

Frances Did I?

Madeleine You reached out your hand.

They both smile at the memory.

'Frances, darling!' Some idiot arriving. 'Frances, you look fabulous.' You and I didn't even touch.

Frances I'm sure.

Madeleine We never shook hands. You turned away.

There is a moment's silence.

I remember making for the door, I rushed for the door, the side door of course. Out by the tradesmen's entrance, and into Bloomsbury, my heart beating fast. Off to a meeting.

Madeleine turns away, overcome at last. Then she moves towards the door.

I'll drive you to the ferry.

Frances Will you? That's kind.

Frances has not moved. Before Madeleine reaches the door, Frances speaks.

What happened was: he saw me in a garden. He walked into a garden and saw me one day. Some birds flew over and the sky was bright blue. I was seventeen. You don't think anything except, 'Here it is.' Because you're young, you've never doubted. You don't even need to expect it. So then when it happens, it's no surprise. The garden's full of people. There's a man, and he's heading towards you with a smile on his face, as if he already knows you.

Frances turns and looks at Madeleine.

When we married I'd never known anyone else.

Frances looks down.

That's why it's now so hard to escape.

Madeleine I think you will.

Frances Do you?

Madeleine Yes.

Frances stands a moment, reluctant to leave.

I'll come with you to the ferry. Then I'm going to walk on the esplanade. Feel the breath of life on my face. (*Madeleine looks round a moment.*) Go down. I'll follow.

Madeleine Thank you.

Frances goes out. You can hear her going down the stairs. Madeleine heads for her computer, but is distracted by the framed photo Frances has left on the desk. She picks it up, looks at it a moment, then opens a drawer and puts it inside. She then closes the drawer, turns off her computer. She calls out.

Hold on. Just coming. Wait for me.

Madeleine goes out. The room stands empty.